KU-477-262

THE WAY I SEE IT
NOW

THE WAY I SEE IT
NOW

by
Cliff Richard

HODDER AND STOUGHTON
LONDON · SYDNEY · AUCKLAND · TORONTO

Copyright © 1968 and 1973 by Cliff Richard. First printed 1968. Sixth impression 1969. Revised edition 1973. ISBN 0 340 16581 2. All rights reserved. No part of this publication may be reproduced or transmitted in any form or by any means, electronic or mechanical, including photocopy, recording, or any information storage and retrieval system, without permission in writing from the publisher. This book is sold subject to the condition that it shall not, by way of trade or otherwise, be lent, re-sold, hired out or otherwise circulated without the publisher's prior consent in any form of binding or cover other than that in which this is published and without a similar condition including this condition being imposed on the subsequent purchaser. Printed in Great Britain for Hodder and Stoughton Limited, St. Paul's House, Warwick Lane, London EC4P 4AH by Richard Clay (The Chaucer Press), Ltd., Bungay, Suffolk.

TO MY MUM

Contents

The Way I See It

Back in 1966 I stood up at a Billy Graham rally and told the audience that I'd become a Christian. It had in fact happened some time before, and had nothing directly to do with Billy Graham, but it seemed a good moment to burn my bridges and get the record straight. From that day on, I've found myself cast in a role I've never asked for, and would happily hand over to anyone else—unofficial spokesman for Christianity. Not only journalists—after all, I've faced them for fourteen years —but vicars, commissions, politicians, sociologists, headmasters, fans and even enemies, have written to me, or interviewed me, or stopped me in the street to ask me my views on just about every imaginable subject remotely connected with religion.

Now I don't mind talking—I hardly ever stop—but as I said in the very first edition of this book, I want to make it clear that I have no special qualifications or genius that makes my opinions any better than anyone else's. Like most people, I've got quite strong opinions about some things. About other things (my taste in clothes, for instance, or even diet) I have views, but I don't hold them very strongly, and they tend to change from time to time. Quite a lot of this book consists of my opinions and views—the way *I* see it—on fairly unimportant matters. Those parts you can take or leave! When this book was first written, it was intended to answer the sort of question I was most frequently asked, and that would certainly include questions about quite trivial and unimportant things. By all means skip those pages if you want to.

But I am also asked—and more and more as time goes by—questions on very important subjects, including what for me is the most important subject of all, *God*. Where I'm dealing with a serious question, I try to give a serious answer. And where I'm dealing with the Christian faith, I try to say what the Bible teaches (as I understand it) rather than simply my "opinion".

The original edition of this book was based on answers to questions thought up by a girl in the publisher's office. Somebody asked her what questions she and her friends would like to put to me if they had the chance. She produced a huge list and I set out to answer them as well as I could. But since then a lot of things have happened about which I'm expected to have an opinion (or a belief!)—the pornography commission, the Festival of Light, "Godspell" and "Jesus Christ Superstar", and the whole "Jesus Movement". And so in this new edition I've tried to answer the usual questions I'm asked about these subjects as well. And I must admit, one or two of my original answers have changed a bit ... not because my basic beliefs have changed (they haven't), but because I'm "x" years older and—perhaps—wiser.

So I hope this book will help to put the record straight about what I think on these and many other subjects. Not because I'm "important", but just so that my friends (and enemies, if I've got any) know why I say and believe what I do.

You can't believe everything you read about me in

the papers, and they don't always get it right when they quote something I'm supposed to have said. But you *can* believe what you read in this book. This *really is* what I believe about silly little things (like science-fiction films) and huge, important things like God, love and being forgiven.

I hope you enjoy it!

1

Getting the Most Out of Life

One day somebody asked me, "Are you scared of death?" Now that's a question you don't get asked too often, so I thought about it.

I enjoy living: that was my first conclusion. I enjoy it very much. If I slipped in the road and a bus was coming at me I'd be gripped by fear. So I enjoy living, and I'm scared of dying; and I guess most other people are, too.

But that didn't answer the question, which was about *death*. And that's a different matter. Dying is something that happens at a certain point in time to all of us. Death is a state we pass into when this life is over.

As a Christian, I'm not worried about, or scared of, death, because I believe God has given to those who believe in Jesus Christ eternal life, that is, life uninterrupted by death. I believe that what lies beyond the end of this life is much better, much more worthwhile than our present lives on earth.

Now that probably seems either a morbid or a very pious way to start a chapter on "getting the most out of life", but I don't think it is. You see, if you know you have *eternal* life, then death shouldn't scare you any longer, and your whole approach to *this* life should be transformed. Honestly, until I became a Christian, I didn't have any idea how happy and satisfying and worthwhile life could be.

I had a good time, of course, and I'm not pretending I was miserable or depressed: but I had a sneaky feeling that there was more to life than I had discovered so far, and that my life then lacked something really vital. Now I know what that "something" was—faith in Jesus Christ, forgiveness and eternal life.

Today, I reckon I'm happier than I've ever been. And I put that down to the difference being a Christian has made. Other things—like drugs, or drink, or even "meditation"—can give you a lift for a while; a sort of shot in the arm. But Jesus Christ can "lift" you permanently. I know, because I have proved it.

Ten years ago I was quite enjoying myself in show-biz—concerts, records, films and all that—but there was this "something" missing. I'd go on stage for half an hour, singing and dancing perhaps, and I'd be quite excited and exhilarated. Then, after the show, we'd all sit about and "wind down", talking about the show, the audience and so on. Gradually, the excitement would wear off, and I'd find myself thinking, "What a drag this all is!" This was before I began even thinking about religion.

Acting, singing, performing, the applause and excitement. This was a sort of drug and, like a drug, it wore off. It was temporary and unreal.

But when I came to Christ I realised what was wrong. I'd been "getting the most out of life", but

selfishly, and not thinking about what I "put into" it.
I saw that whatever gifts I had been given had been
given by God and should be offered back to Him and
used for Him.

Now I still do the same sort of things—making records, films, singing and so on—not for a temporary
kick, but "for God", to His glory. At least, that is
what I aim at. And that way, it isn't any longer a question of "getting the most out of life" but of giving our
lives to God and letting Him fill them and make them
satisfying and real.

Of course, this doesn't mean a Christian can't enjoy
ordinary human pleasures. In fact, I think I enjoy
them much more—or most of them—nowadays.

I've always loved pop and a little jazz music. Actually, my favourite female singer is a jazz artist. But I
like beat music and the "big band" sound, too. I think
the reason I was so keen on rock 'n roll back in the
fifties was that it combined a strong beat with the
spontaneous element of jazz. In rock 'n roll the com-
poser works out the words and music, the arranger
shapes the whole thing, but the performer makes it
come alive—with shouts, yelps of delight and so on! I
still prefer to sing "up tempo" numbers.

I'm a real film fan. I particularly like a good musical
(like "West Side Story") or science fiction—you
know, bug-eyed monsters and all that. Don't ask me
why! When I used to be on tour with the Shadows
with an afternoon on our hands, we'd look up the local
paper and find out where they were showing a really

ghastly horror or science-fiction film—like "The Fifty Foot Woman" or "Thirteen Ghosts" (where they gave the audience red and green pairs of spectacles—you looked through the green pair if you wanted to see the ghosts!). Then we'd all go along and loll in the stalls lapping it up. They were terrible films but great fun.

I like biblical films and epics. "The Greatest Story Ever Told" was very good and easily my favourite, until I saw Pasolini's "The Gospel According to Saint Matthew". That film, although only in black and white, and without spectacle, really got through to me —I felt this must have been what it was "really like". I enjoyed "Nicholas and Alexandra", too, perhaps because it explored two interesting, sensitive people and their relationship. "Fiddler on the Roof" was enjoyable, as well—it was wholesome ... you came out feeling clean, which is quite a change in the cinema nowadays.

Now I know that makes me sound like a middle-aged prude, but the fact is that for a film "fan" like me it's really become quite hard to find films that one can enjoy without being offended by them. I found "The Devils" literally disgusting. It seemed sick that the subject should ever have been filmed. But even there I found the portrait of the priest very inspiring. He believed, and he was prepared to die for his beliefs. "Straw Dogs" I also found ugly. The last half-hour was really vicious. Perhaps the most disturbing thing was that when the "hero" turned on his tormentors with this terribly exaggerated, extreme violence, I found myself actually enjoying it. I think that shows how subtle and dangerous the whole "permissive" thing is. We all, perhaps unconsciously, adjust to new —lower?—standards. But I'll come back to that subject in a later chapter.

You may well ask why I go to see films which I must know I'm going to find offensive or disgusting. Well, in some cases you *don't* know in advance, especially if you go to a pre-release or première showing. But in other cases, I've known that I would certainly be asked for my opinions about certain films, and I don't believe it's right to pass opinions about films or shows that I haven't actually seen. For people who don't *have* to see them my honest advice is, don't. Some people justify them by saying that they deal with "real life", and to ignore them is to shut one's eyes to "real life". Don't you believe it! These films— ones like "The Devils" and "Straw Dogs"—don't deal with "real life" as most of us know it. They deal with a very rare and odd and distorted kind of "real life", which, please God, you'll never have to face in reality. The fact that I enjoy films doesn't mean that I've got to force myself to enjoy nightmares, too.

I think my love of films (which doesn't extend to stage plays very often) and the sort of films I usually like comes from an enjoyment of illusion. (That's not true of "Bonnie and Clyde", of course!) Films create an illusion for me that stage plays hardly ever do. Even working on films, walking over sets and appreciating the techniques involved in filming hasn't destroyed the sense of illusion.

In case you're thinking that's probably true of my religion, too, and that it's all an illusion, I want to make it clear that faith in Jesus Christ is the most realistic thing that has happened to me. As I hope to show in this book, it has opened my eyes to things I'd never seen before, made me face up to things I would sooner not have thought about, and do and say things where I'd sooner do nothing or keep silent. *This isn't illusion*. Jesus Christ for me is the only *real* Person who ever lived. That's why following Him is the way to become a real person yourself, and find out what life is really all about.

2

All You Need is Love

I reckon there's a lot of nonsense talked about sex. The biggest bit of nonsense is the idea that Christians are "against" it.

To Christians, as to everybody else, sex is very important. But for Christians it is also a sacred thing, which can only be enjoyed and properly shared with one person. This is what God planned from the beginning. The Bible is not against sex, but it is against sex misused. Sex outside marriage, for instance, is always wrong: that is what the Bible calls "fornication".

The reason is that sex is not a "thing" on its own, but part of a deep human relationship planned by God. He said that it "was not good for man to be alone". He said that a man and his wife become "one flesh"—one person, really. Sex detached from God's plan is sex wasted on a substitute.

This deep human relationship in marriage is based on love, and sex is part—an important part—of it.

Like most people, I'd like to get married. In fact, I've never considered that I might not. I don't consciously go about thinking, "I must get married", but I never contemplate a life of bachelorhood (despite that song "Bachelor Boy"!).

I suppose I could have been married long ago, but two things have held me back and, as they illustrate what I've just been saying, I would like to explain them carefully.

The first is the whole idea of "love". Everybody uses the word and sings about it, but the strange thing is very few couples tell you straight, "We're in love." They say, "We're going steady," or something like that. It's almost as though they're ashamed of being in love.

Now, *why*?

Have we used the word loosely for so long that we don't believe the real thing exists? I, for one, would rather not be married at all than have a marriage without love. I mean that, and that's one reason I have held back to make sure.

The second is the whole idea of marriage. According to the Bible, marriage is a permanent, lifelong union: the two people become one, forming the whole basis of family life, bringing up children and so on. Whether people stay in love or not is an individual matter, but marriage, the way God intended it, is permanent. If two people just can't live together, then separation may be essential, but that can't end the marriage, according to the words of Jesus.

This is the thing that worries me. Most of the people who have been through the divorce courts have sincerely tried in their marriage, and it simply hasn't worked for them. What frightens me most of all is the thought that after, say, five or six years of marriage, I should find that I couldn't love my wife. Believing marriage to be permanent, there would be no final way out of the situation.

At the same time, marriage, and love and sex in marriage, isn't meant to be a matter for fear or doubt. It's just that it is so important that the most stupid thing is to treat it casually.

I think it is important to be sure one loves the person one is going to marry, because marriage is such a big step, choosing a lifelong partner. Unfortunately, some people—especially some men—treat this subject almost as a big joke. Some even go into it thinking, "Well, if it doesn't work out, we'll get a divorce." Others, having got into marriage, ignore the vows they have made and carry on with somebody else. Some men claim that it is a man's prerogative to be promiscuous—to have sex whenever and wherever he can. Personally, I think this is the *worst* quality any man could have, because it is misusing one of God's *best* gifts.

It is because I feel strongly that one should be sure about one's partner before getting married that I broke with the one girl I've met so far whom I seriously thought of marrying. It wasn't that I "went off her", but that I reckoned doubts were no basis for marriage, and so we parted. It wasn't easy, but I reckon it was a lot easier than an unsuccessful marriage or a broken home years later.

I think a good attitude to love, marriage and sex should start when we're quite young, and show itself in a sensible, balanced approach to the opposite sex. Personally, the main quality I like to see in a girl is reserve. I don't mean by that that her personality should be obliterated. Many girls think that no one will notice them if they're quiet, but I must say I hate girls who are too forward. For myself—and I think this is true of almost all men—if I like a girl then I must make the first move. I should like to feel that I took the first step towards getting to know her. If they only realised it, it's the pushing, aggressive girls who put boys off, and the quieter, more reserved ones who attract their attention.

There is no doubt that a healthy approach to love and sex is a great asset in life. For me, the standards have been laid down once and for all by God in the Bible. I believe that to break those standards is to ruin your chance of happiness. But to keep them is to find the best way—*God's* way—to happiness and fulfilment.

3

Who's the Greatest?

The greatest man who ever lived? I wonder who your choice would be? For me, there's only one possible answer—Jesus Christ. And I want to explain why.

Jesus Christ lived on earth about two thousand years ago, and we've got plenty of evidence about His life. Not even a cynic or atheist can deny that Jesus Christ existed as a man and that during His life He did some fantastic things. Christianity is not based on feelings and emotions but on *facts*.

There came the time when the authorities turned against Jesus, and so did some of the people. He was arrested and put to death, a very cruel death by crucifixion. His followers—the disciples—eleven of them, ran away frightened and hid themselves in an upper room. They had seen Christ crucified, and it looked as though that was the end of the action.

But those frightened disciples suddenly, a few weeks later, got their nerve back and marched into the streets of Jerusalem as bold as brass, saying that Jesus had risen from the dead.

Now, what could have changed them if that wasn't true? They went on to turn the world upside down *because Jesus Christ was alive again*. There's no other explanation for it, and nobody has ever produced one.

You can't argue against the Person of Christ. He is real, and He is alive.

Of course, the cynic won't accept that.

"Oh, He was a very good man. If He'd been alive today He'd have made a big mark. He probably had a good public relations man . . ."

All right. So Jesus Christ was a "very good" man. Most people will agree that He was one of the best men who ever lived.

But this "good, *very* good" man also claimed to be the Son of God. He actually said it, not once but several times. The High Priest asked Him directly once, "Are you the Christ, the Son of the Blessed?" Jesus answered, "I am." Now that's pretty clear, isn't it?

"Ah yes," said the cynic, "but perhaps He was mad, or deluded, or a liar."

But could someone who was mad, or a liar, have spoken the Sermon on the Mount, which everyone looks up to as tremendous, brilliant and *good*?

As I see it, you can't get away from the fact that Jesus Christ *is* the Son of God, as He claimed, and *is* alive today.

I believe He is alive now—the greatest man who ever lived—and alive in every sense. He was a man like us, except that He never sinned; and He is divine, the Son of God. His mother was a woman, a human; His Father is God. What a Person!

He died, but He has risen from the dead. He appeared to His followers—not in exactly the same form as before, but obviously alive. He appeared to a man called Saul outside Damascus—a man who had been persecuting the Church but who became Saint Paul, the great Christian evangelist.

This is how Christ is alive—coming to people and speaking to them and changing their lives. That is how I know He is alive: He has come to me and spoken to me and changed my life. I wouldn't be writing this now if I didn't know He was alive. I can say I "know" Him, because He has changed my life: not suddenly, like Saint Paul, but over a period of a couple of years.

Now why do I say this Jesus Christ is the greatest man who ever lived? Not only because He is the Son of God. Not only because He rose from the dead and is alive now. But because of the fantastic things He has done and can do *for us*. You see, the living Jesus Christ offers us tremendous things.

He offers us forgiveness of our sins. I'm going to say some more about that later on; but it is a tremendous thing to have our sins forgiven.

He offers us eternal life—immortality. The Bible says, "God gave us eternal life, and this life is in His Son. He who has the Son has life; he who has not the Son has not life."* What an utterly fantastic thing— that Jesus Christ offers human beings immortality, eternal life.

I believe He is the greatest because He has done the greatest things—not for Himself but for us. He died

* 1 John 5:11, 12 (RSV).

for us; He lives *in* us, if we believe in Him. I believe anyone who reads the New Testament and gets to know this wonderful Person will not find Him boring, and they won't be able to ignore Him. He is really irresistible: a tremendous personality, kind but strong, powerful but gentle; utterly good. You really ought to get to know Him!

Not For Me!

Some people seem to think that all pop singers are main-lining narcotics and everybody in showbiz is stoned to the eyebrows. Perhaps that's why just about every other person I meet asks for my opinion on drug-taking.

In fact, I only know about it from what I've read in the papers and seen on television, so don't expect expert comments!

Of course, I have met pop singers and other entertainers who take drugs, and even some who are addicted, but I can honestly say I've seen very little of it. I heard of one girl singer who had to be given a "shot" before she went on TV, to see her through the show. But, in my view, it is not the stars who go in for drugs, but the near-misses and failures who are compensating for their lack of success. Of course, there are exceptions. But, from my experience, show business is so demanding, and everything you do is so exposed to the public, that really well-known artists would soon flop if they became addicted. I think we have seen that happen in some cases. I feel that the work of some famous artists has obviously deteriorated since they got mixed up with drug-taking. Unfortunately, performers who take drugs often think their performance is improved, but, in fact, they are terrible but too stoned to know it!

The way I see it, people turn to drugs to fill a gap. There is a need unfulfilled: they find life unsatisfying, or else it's got on top of them. Sometimes, perhaps, they are after "kicks"—something *different*, more exciting, to lift life out of a rut.

But what drugs offer is really a lie. They don't actually change anything; they certainly don't alter your circumstances or change your life, except for the worse. And whatever help they give does not last.

I think that's the really terrible thing about drugs. They give you a lift for a moment and then leave you worse off than you were before: they are just a temporary crutch and, when it's taken away, you fall flat on your face.

Then, there doesn't seem to be any doubt that they have other bad effects. They ruin your health, turn you into a sort of zombie and, in many cases, finally cause death.

Now that's a pretty long list of bad results to set against the gain of a temporary "kick", isn't it? On one side, a few hours of feeling "high" and forgetting your troubles: on the other the horrible drop when it wears off, the wrecking of your health, the loss of normal joy in living and even, for those who are crazy enough to get badly hooked, death. That sounds like every sort of a bad bargain to me. Honestly, plain *logic* wouldn't allow me to take drugs, even if I couldn't see any moral objection to them. Taking narcotics is a mug's game: everything to pay, and nothing permanent to show for it.

From the horrible mess it seems to make of people's lives, it is hard to understand how people can allow themselves to become addicted in the first place. I suppose, in their terrible need or loneliness or depression, they just don't think about the bad consequences. I really feel very sorry for them.

Of course, for a Christian there are other good reasons for keeping well clear of drugs. Two of them impress me a lot.

The first is this. If you take narcotics, you will almost certainly become addicted to them. That means that you can't possibly get by without taking drugs in larger and larger doses. Many young people think they are exceptional and can take these drugs without getting "hooked". But it's too late when you find you're an addict to wish you had never risked it. The addict is in a pitiful condition and deserves all our help and sympathy: but the fact remains that many, many addicts have gone in with their eyes wide open, refusing to listen to warnings from teachers, parents or friends.

Now for a Christian to run the risk of becoming addicted is sheer disobedience. If you're hooked on drugs you're a slave to them—literally. They own your life: you live for the next "shot". But a Christian is described in the Bible as a "slave" of Jesus Christ. He runs our lives: we live for Him. Jesus warned us that we can't possibly serve two masters. You certainly can't be a slave to heroin *and* Christ. Simply put, taking narcotics can't be good if you can't possibly do without them, because then you are a slave to them.

Of course, we can become addicted to other "drugs"—fame, money, success, sex. There are plenty of people who are hooked on these just as definitely as others are hooked on narcotics, and it's just as evil. Even quite harmless things, like going to the pictures, can become a drug to us—the films used to be for me. I went twice a week at one time, and could easily have got hooked. That doesn't sound bad, but for a Christian, being a slave to anything or anyone but Christ is a sin, a serious sin.

The second reason is more positive. I said that most people take drugs because there is a gap in their life; it isn't satisfying them, or it's got on top of them, or they're looking for some extra kick of pleasure or excitement.

But a Christian shouldn't have this sort of gap. Life for the Christian is meant to be satisfying and balanced. I must say that there is just no comparison between the joy I now have as a Christian and the pleasure I got from life before I turned to Christ. Jesus Christ is the One to fill the gaps, to give satisfaction and purpose and to enable us to cope with the problems and burdens that get on top of us. He is the "extra" for real living, too.

I realise some people have bigger burdens and problems than I've ever known, and I don't pretend Christians don't have their share of these darker things. I can't say I know the answer to depression or doubt. But I do know this, it definitely *doesn't* lie in a syringe or a pill box—not the permanent answer. And it definitely *does* lie in God, somehow, somewhere.

For people in normal circumstances, Jesus Christ can and does fill that gap of emptiness in life. The way I see it, He is the only permanent answer to the needs drugs answer only temporarily.

One other thing about drugs seems important to me.

Some youngsters have started to take drugs because over the last couple of years it has become the "fashion". In some circles, if you don't take drugs, or at least pretend to, you're regarded as being an outcast. It's come to be regarded by some youngsters as clever to be on drugs—as if there's anything clever in slowly addling your brain, ruining your body and killing yourself by slow stages!

But if this has become a fashion, then those who set the fashion have a lot to answer for. People in the public eye, like pop singers and so on, can't pretend they don't influence their fans. They *do*, for good or evil. I believe we have a moral responsibility to set *good* fashions, and will have to answer one day for any people we have led astray.

That leads me to something that worries me quite a lot. I'm afraid that one day somebody may see something I do, or hear about it—something bad or unhelpful—and say, "He calls himself a Christian, and look what he's done," and be turned away from God because of me.

That's what I mean by moral responsibility. Every Christian has it, but if you are well known and everything you do is seized upon and publicised, then the responsibility is greater. It's not possible to take all the advantages of being popular and successful without also incurring responsibilities. For me, the chief responsibility is that if I slip up, Christ's name is blasphemed. I can honestly say that this thought worries me all the time.

I've called this chapter "Not for me", but so far I have only talked about drugs. However, there are a few more things that I personally would rather be without.

One of them is tobacco. I must admit I have always hated smoking, which seems to me one of the most unnatural things humans have ever done. To inhale dirty smoke into lungs made to take clean air seems to me an odd way to get pleasure. However, that's just a matter of taste. I've never liked it and never been tempted to take up smoking, so I suppose I may be a bit smug about it. There was a time when I nearly vomited if I had to handle an ash-tray.

I'm not saying it is a serious sin to smoke, or anything like that. I think it's unhygienic and, so far as I understand what the experts say, it also seems to have been proved that it's very bad for your health and can often lead to lung cancer.

Rather like the situation with drugs, it seems daft to

me to accept a few minutes' pleasure from a cigarette in exchange for a few years of your life.

I think most youngsters start smoking to be "one of the boys", and then they get hooked: and it does seem like a mild form of addiction. From then on they spend a terrible amount of money ruining their health.

For the Christian, I think smoking should be discouraged on two counts. It's a great waste of money, and it makes you a slave to tobacco. The mere fact that countless people try hard to give it up, but fail, proves to me that they are slaves to smoking. As we saw with drugs, if you are a slave to something else, you can't be a faithful "slave" to Jesus Christ. There are those who say they can give smoking up at any time. Then why not give it up? After all, every smoker I've ever met tells me what a lousy habit it is!

I think it is rather different with drinking—though that may be just because, whereas I hate smoking, I do like an occasional glass of wine or something. But I think the difference is that drinking is a natural thing (that is, everybody has to drink something), whereas smoking is basically unnatural. After all, Jesus Christ drank alcoholic drinks, so if it was all right for the Son of God, I guess it's all right for me, too!

But that's not the whole picture. After all, Jesus Christ was the perfect Man. There was no question of His drinking to excess or getting drunk. But with us it's different.

The way I see it, if you can control it, it's all right. If it controls you, it's out. Moderation is the thing—

can I use my sense, control myself, keep it in perspective?

But it honestly would not bother me if I never touched another drop of alcohol. For me, the best drink in the world is a cold orange squash. And certainly if by drinking alcohol I was putting temptation in somebody's way—say, making it harder for an alcoholic to resist having a drink—I'd avoid drinking altogether. The Bible says, "Do not give way to drunkenness and the dissipation that goes with it, but let the Holy Spirit fill you."* That seems to me to set the Christian standard. Drunkenness—when the alcohol takes control—is *out*. And the positive thing is that the Christian can be filled by the Holy Spirit and be under His control instead.

* Ephesians 5 : 18 (NEB).

5

The Bomb, and All That

Nowadays entertainers, pop stars and musicians are all
expected to have political views, so it's not surprising
that I'm often asked what I think about politics, the
Government, the H-bomb, racial strife and other
questions like these. I have no special knowledge, and
neither have most of the other showbiz people who go
on about these things, but for some reason it is expected that we should say our bit.

Before I became a Christian, I was completely indifferent to politics. I was busy doing my job and, I
suppose, thought, "I'm all right, Jack."

Now I have changed my attitude. I believe Christians should care about the way the country is run.
The Bible says all power is put there by God anyway,* whether the Government is a good one or a bad
one. In fact, Jesus Christ told Pontius Pilate, who was
about to decide whether to let Him be put to death or
not, that the power Pilate had was "given to him from
above". We are told to pray for "kings and all who are
in high positions",† and I reckon they need all the
help they can get nowadays. If the early Christians
prayed for the Roman Emperor and Government,

* Romans 13 : 1.
† 1 Timothy 2 : 2 (RSV).

who were busy persecuting them, then there's no reason why we shouldn't pray for our Government, even if we happen to support the Opposition!

But it doesn't end with praying for them. I don't think we can just say a prayer for the people who run the country, and then wash our hands of all responsibility for it. The big thing is to decide just what we ought to do. Some people think that if you don't demonstrate, sit outside embassies or get yourself arrested in Downing Street obstructing the police, you're indifferent to what is going on in the world. Now I'm as worried as the next person about the state of the world and our own country, but for me that doesn't seem to be the answer.

God gives different gifts to different people. Some are called by Him to get involved in politics and government and, if they are, He gives them what they need to do it. I'm quite sure that, whatever gifts God has given me, mine don't lie in this field! I can't get madly interested in it, I must admit, but I *do* think it is important.

In a democracy, every adult has the right to vote, and I believe it is a duty to do so. But it's often very hard for a Christian to decide for whom to vote. Some people say, "Vote for the Christian candidate." In fact, often there is no Christian standing in a constituency: but even if there is, there's another problem. If I vote for a Christian candidate, ignoring his party, I am voting for his party and its views, because by and large he has to vote with his party. After all, he can't run the country on his own! So really I am voting for a party and its policies, rather than for an individual.

All the same, I think I would still vote for the Christian candidate. A Christian politician should be more prepared to say, "I obey my conscience," rather than just do what the party leaders tell him.

So I think a definite Christian would get my vote. If there were no Christian standing, I should try to study the policies of the different parties at the time of the election and then decide which one most nearly represented my views or was nearest to the Christian position.

There's one other thing about politics that seems important to me. Some people seem to imply that, if only we could get wars stopped, H-bombs banned and so on, the world would be perfect. I think the "flower people" take this view—if we could all just "love one another" everything would be wonderful.

To me, this is unrealistic. It doesn't face up to the facts about human nature. *Of course* I want to see wars stopped. *Of course* I believe people should love each other. But you don't put an end to hatred, violence and greed just by negotiation, or by going around waving flowers and saying "love is all". The problem goes deep, so the answer must go deep.

The Bible says that all of these evil things start *inside* man, in human nature. Jesus said that "out of *the heart* come evil thoughts, murder, adultery" and so on. Wars are just a large-scale version of individual

sin. It starts in man's heart, and it's got to be put right
there. Until people are right, the world won't be right.

Not only that, but Jesus said that there would be
wars "and rumours of wars" right up until the time
when He would return. I don't believe that there will
ever be perfect peace and happiness on earth until
after Jesus Christ has come back. That doesn't mean
we shouldn't do all we can to prevent wars and limit
suffering. God doesn't want people to suffer, and we
can pray and work for peace. But if we are realists, we
must face the facts, and the facts are that, human
nature being what it is, there will always be hatred,
greed and violence. It is one of the awful results of
man being in rebellion against God, and of man's
heart being corrupted by sin. We won't change that by
waving banners, or flowers. We can help by praying,
by telling people that Jesus Christ can change their
hearts; and we can get involved in helping in practical
ways to prevent war and suffering, or to limit its
effects.

Of course, the world would be a much better place
if everybody lived according to the teaching of Christ
—in the Sermon on the Mount, for instance—turning the other cheek, loving their enemies and so on.
But, to me, that sounds like the kingdom of God, and
that won't come until the King (Jesus) comes.

Christians should try to meet need and help people
because Christ commanded us to do so. But our
greatest help is to bring them to Christ and to eternal
life. At the same time, Christians try to care about

people and their problems, whereas by nature human beings are basically selfish.

I remember when I was at work in the office of a factory as a youngster, getting £4. 15s. a week, we used to say that if everybody gave just a shilling to relieve the starving or homeless, we would still have £4. 14s. left and hardly miss the odd shilling—but what a difference it would make to them! But as a Christian, I still feel so frustrated: so much could be done, but people don't seem to care. It's *people* who need to be changed!

So it's not that I don't *care* about wars, the bomb and suffering, but that, because of what the Bible teaches, I can't accept simple answers to deep problems—problems that cannot be solved apart from God.

6

The Jesus Movement

I suppose it was in about 1970 that we started hearing about the "Jesus Movement" in the States—the Jesus Freaks, the Jesus Communes and so on. It all sounded very exciting, with news of hundreds of thousands of kids "turning on to Jesus", many of them giving up drugs and giving their lives to Christ. As time has gone on, we've learnt more—and the "movement" has come to Britain and other parts of Europe. We've learnt to distinguish between groups like the "Children of God", who have all the marks of a "sect", denouncing everybody else, living in communes and demanding absolute obedience from their members, and people like Arthur Blessitt, who works with and even sometimes *in* the existing churches. I met Arthur Blessitt at a big conference on Evangelism, and was very struck by his ability to "relate" to people, and his tremendous warmth and friendliness. At the same time, I was amazed at the amount of religious "jargon" he used. Many of the "Jesus People" have gone back to the King James ("Authorised") Version of the Bible—perhaps that's the religious equivalent of some of the antique gear preferred by customers in the King's Road and Carnaby Street!

I don't expect the Jesus Movement to catch on in

Britain in the same way as it has in the States—though I think there will be a "movement" towards Jesus Christ here. In fact, I think it's begun already. But I think two things will make it different here. In the first place, I don't think the British are as emotional about their religion as Americans, especially Californians, where this all began. Or, if we are as emotional, we hide it better. Secondly, I don't think our young people are such enthusiastic "joiners" as young Americans. They don't like being regimented, or told what to do, or urged to join this or that. Perhaps they're just a bit more cynical. Whatever it is, it's hard to imagine hundreds of thousands of British young people trooping along chanting identical slogans and reciting verses from the Bible out loud together.

I'm not criticising the American movement in saying that. Any "movement" that brings the name of Jesus back into prominence must be good ... anywhere in the world. I think that perhaps the Festival of Light may become our British Jesus Movement. It certainly seems to be moving that way.

Many people have associated the Jesus Movement with the stage shows "Godspell" and "Jesus Christ Superstar", though in fact the connection is the other way round. I think that the *fact* of the Jesus Movement brought the name and life and teaching of Jesus back into prominence, and that in turn meant that writers and composers began to think again of Jesus as a suitable subject for their work. After all, he was the *main* subject of artists six hundred years ago.

In fact, there is an enormous difference between "Godspell" and "Superstar", which many people seem to have missed. "Superstar" is not a Christian piece. We have the word of its creators for that. They didn't set out to write a Christian opera, but one based on the "Jesus story". In fact, it is a very free, human interpretation of *part* of the Jesus story—seen through the eyes of Judas. I suppose I'm not a "heavy" music fan, so it's hard for me to comment on it fairly as a rock opera, but from the Christian point of view it is thoroughly misleading. Some of the songs are good, but even in the best of them ("I Don't Know How to Love Him") we have a line that says that Jesus is "a man, just a man". Now Mary Magdalene may well have felt that at one time, but it does in fact sum up the view of the whole piece. Certainly "Superstar" cannot in any sense be seen as part of the Jesus Movement, though I don't think it would have had the success it has if it hadn't been for the Jesus Movement putting Jesus back into the headlines.

"Godspell" is very different. I don't think anyone could become a Christian through seeing "Superstar", but they could through seeing "Godspell". "Godspell" provides the basic material for a faith, because it presents a biblical picture of Jesus. It's not the *whole* picture—but what sermon gives the whole picture? It doesn't show very clearly *why* Jesus died, for instance. But then there isn't much about that in St Matthew's Gospel, either, on which it is based. "Godspell" is the only "showbiz" presentation of Christ we have had that is true to the New Testament, even though it more or less restricts itself to the teachings of Jesus and his crucifixion. About the resurrection, which is the cornerstone of Christianity, it is a bit indecisive. I think even the cast have changed their views on this! At first they argued that the resurrection was there musically but not dramatically, as it couldn't be portrayed visually. Now they seem to be saying that it *is* there visually, in so far as "Jesus" joins the rest of the cast back on stage for the final reprise of "Day by Day". But I don't think the ordinary spectator would feel that the Jesus who is carried away to burial (through the audience) comes "alive again".

I've seen "Godspell" four times, and I can honestly say that it's seemed better each time. If you know the Gospels pretty well, you get much more "out" of it, because it is very subtle and even profound at times. The writer obviously knew the Gospels inside out— and *understood* them, what's more. I wasn't all that struck with the music, but it does grow on you.

I've been interested to see the impact that "Godspell" has had on the cast. I've talked to them several times since the show opened, and they almost all admit that the effect of reciting the words of Jesus night after night has been to change their attitude not just to him but to life. Their reaction is to remark on how consistent it is, and what good sense it all makes when you really begin to see what Jesus was driving at. Funny, but that's what Christian preachers have been saying for centuries!

As well as shows like "Godspell" and "Superstar", we've also had scores of records, many of them in the charts, with strong Christian themes. Again, I don't think this is part of the Jesus Movement, but with Jesus in the news, the pop-song writers have turned their attention to him as well. Not only that, but somebody discovered that some old hymns have got really strong melodies, and so we've had hits like "Amazing Grace" and "Happy Day", which are simply updated versions of hymns that have been popular with Christians for generations. Of course this isn't surprising. A good tune is a good tune, and if it's become a "standard" with people in church there's no reason why it shouldn't also become a "standard" with people outside church, too. Look how football crowds pick up the old hymn tunes and put their own words to them.

As well as the old hymns updated, we've also had a lot of completely new songs in the charts with Christian themes. Artists like Ray Stevens have made them a staple part of their output—though Ray has also used old, well-loved Christian hymns and choruses. You couldn't get a much more directly Christian song than "Turn Your Radio On". Funnily enough, however, I've not had all that much success with directly Christian songs. When I sing them it's "propaganda", apparently. Still, all of this talking and singing and arguing about Jesus works for good in the long run where the Christian cause is concerned. At least it ensures that he doesn't get ignored!

7

Isn't Church Boring?

During a long run in "Cinderella" at the London Palladium I was asked, "What is your favourite thing at the moment?"

I answered, "Sundays". This was quoted in a magazine article and it surprised a lot of people, I believe.

At that time, my week was hectic. People don't realise how hard you work during a show like that. I was at the theatre six days a week from lunch-time until about eleven, and hardly ever got into bed until the early hours of the morning.

On Sundays, everything was different. A quiet relaxed Sunday dinner, then off to Crusaders—the Bible class where I'm an assistant leader—tea with a few friends perhaps, and then off to evening service at church and afterwards the Youth Fellowship meeting in the church hall, with guitars out and some really good singing!

To some people, that may sound like the biggest drag on record. In fact, I meant it when I said it was "my favourite thing". I can't believe anybody "living it up" in the West End could possibly get the satisfaction I do from an ordinary, quiet, routine Sunday *as a Christian*.

EAST ANGLIAN DAILY TIMES & ASSOCIATED PAPERS

WILLIAM WORSFOLD

CLIFFORD SHIRLEY

CLIFFORD SHIRLEY

EDWARD LEIGH

EDWARD LEIGH

"But," people say, "isn't church dull and boring? All those dreary hymns and psalms, dark buildings and empty pews?"

I used to think so, I admit, before I became a Christian. It's looking at it with Christian eyes that makes the difference.

We all know church services could have things "injected" into them to make them more interesting; but I think this should only be done to help non-Christians not to feel strange when they come to a service. That, for me, is the only justification for having "beat" music and so on in church.

For Christians, we shouldn't need entertaining in church. We go to worship God, not to be entertained. Church services are for God, not for us. Of course, this doesn't mean we are complacent about the dull and drab services that are all too common. Clergymen with dead voices, tuneless hymns, psalm chants nobody can follow and drab buildings are some of the things I find hard to endure. And something can, and should, be done about them.

Some people criticise the robes that the clergy or the choir wear, and things like that. I agree, these things can make it all seem a bit medieval. Special robes don't worry me—they add to the atmosphere of reverence for me: but I realise that the "outsider" may be put off by them, and others will always regard them as weird.

Here is where something Paul says in the Bible*

* See Romans 14:1.

becomes important. He talks about not causing the "weaker brother" to stumble by disputes about "opinions". He explains that one Christian will prefer one way of expressing his devotion to Christ, and another will prefer another way. Neither should cause offence to the other.

With things like robes, I believe we should answer the question, "Why do you have to dress like that?" by saying, "We don't *have* to—other Christians don't." There are, after all, plenty of churches where the minister conducts the service dressed in a lounge suit. Nobody should stay away from church for a reason like that. Some of us are helped by a more formal sort of service : others are helped by an informal approach; in the same way, not everybody likes the same kind of music.

I think people raise these trivial things as excuses for staying away from church and won't listen when Christians try to answer them. The truth is, they don't know what they're missing!

Sometimes I'm asked what I feel about Holy Communion.

Actually, I had been a Christian quite a good time before I really thought about it very much.

I was attending Confirmation classes at my church, but I couldn't quite see what being allowed to join in the Communion service would add to my Christian life. We had twelve sessions with the vicar, and I think it was in the eighth session that he was talking about the Communion service. Suddenly, I realised that what the vicar—Paul Betts—was saying made sense. This service is a wonderful way to get really close to Jesus Christ and to let him become part of me.

Now, for me, the Communion service (or Lord's Supper) is a very personal thing. It gives a tremendous feeling of sharing in Christ and sharing Him with my fellow-Christians at the service. Salvation doesn't depend on going to Communion, as some people seem to suggest, but it *is* a very important part of the Christian life.

What is "church" anyway? That's something I've often thought about. It isn't really a building or an organisation. It is the Christian *family* meeting together. Paul wrote his letters in the New Testament to congregations or groups of Christians in different places. So the church is just a number of Christians in one place, coming together like a family, to worship God.

Church is "home", too, for the Christian. For me, that means family loyalty is involved. It won't do to go from church to church, trying to find one that "suits" you, or just for a change. Loyalty to the family means being committed to one group of Christians in one place.

The different denominations bother some people, but they don't worry me very much. I'm an Anglican, but I prefer to describe myself to non-Christians simply as a Christian. If I say I'm an Anglican, they'll just drag up everything they can think of against the Church of England as an excuse for rejecting Christ—

the Church Commissioners, church parades in the Army, the vicar on TV and so on. But if I say "I'm a Christian", they find it much harder to pick holes in Christ!

Denominations are just labels on groups of Christians who worship in different ways or believe differently about some secondary matters. But all true Christians are united under one Leader, Jesus Christ. Our religion has a living Head, not a dead hero, as its founder, and we are "all one in Christ Jesus".

So you see, I do *not* find church dull or boring. Seen through Christian eyes, it is the family of God's people, where we learn and worship and work together. You won't believe how satisfying and exciting that can be—until you have come in and joined us!

8

Light, and Darkness

One of the things to have come to the front lately has been the whole question of "permissiveness", and especially where books, plays and films are concerned. When I was asked to join Lord Longford's Commission on Pornography, I was forced to think about my attitude to this. As I joined in the discussions, and read some of the masses of paper produced by the various working groups, my thinking became a lot clearer, though obviously there are enormous problems.

In the first place, there is one thing about which Malcolm Muggeridge has convinced me, and that is that Christians must be categorical. There *is* a line to be drawn. We may argue about exactly where and how it should be drawn, but we must surely agree that some things are absolutely right, and some things are absolutely wrong. While we argue over the grey areas, others are exploiting the black ones.

Of course we can't foist Christian standards on those who don't even believe that God exists. But if we know, as we do, that certain things will bring God's judgment, and that other things inevitably bring appalling consequences (like drug addiction, or venereal disease), are we really being kind to people by being silent when we should be shouting out a warning? I like Malcolm Muggeridge simply because he is so definite. Of course he exaggerates at times. I suppose everybody does. But not many Christians are prepared nowadays to take the unpopular stand of saying that certain activities are totally wrong, and should be totally condemned.

But what can we do about it? It is one thing to say that obscene books, for instance, are evil. It is quite another to decide what a mixed Christian and non-Christian society can be expected to do about it. At the moment we can't even agree on a definition of what "obscenity" actually is, even though I reckon most of us instinctively know when we meet it. And while we argue about the borderline cases, really revolting obscenity, which everybody (except those making money out of it) would condemn, is taking place—things like films of intercourse with babies or animals.

So, what can we do? In a democracy you've got to carry the majority with you if you want to stop anything by law. It's no good simply shouting that something is "unChristian". We've got to show that it's harmful, and we've got to convince at least a majority of our fellow-countrymen that it's harmful. We've got to carry them with us, not conquer them. At the moment, they simply react to people like Lord Longford and Malcolm Muggeridge—and Mary Whitehouse—by asking "Who do you think you are, telling me how to behave?" But if we could convince them that what we deplore is the evil results of certain things—evil for *everybody*, that is, Christian and non-Christian—then we may get somewhere.

But we must be categorical. Of that I'm sure. There *is* a line, an absolute right and wrong. We live in an extreme world—extremely violent, extremely prejudiced. We can't always afford to be "moderate". Perversions tend to become stronger all the while. As I was saying earlier, our standards do tend to slip all the while, even when we think we are "making a stand". There will be no limit at all unless we *do* something, and do it soon. I realise that censorship won't stop obscenity, any more than laws stop sin. But it may limit it. And if there's one thing I've learnt sitting on the Pornography Commission, it's that we must find a way, and soon, to limit the spread of pornography. I don't think we should make moral decisions for other adults, but it has become a question of protecting the next generation.

For all those reasons, I gave my support to the Nationwide Festival of Light, though I was not, despite any impressions you may have gained to the contrary, one of its leading figures. I had nothing to do with its planning, but I was happy to appear at various Festival activities. I've been even happier since the movement took on a more positively Christian line. As I've said, I think it might become the British "Jesus Movement", supported by masses of young people and reaching out on the streets and in other places to win youngsters for Christ.

Certainly, recently I have found a fantastic change

for the better in the reaction of kids at schools and students to the Christian faith. I travel around a lot talking and singing in schools and colleges. I've been doing this for six or seven years, and I can honestly say that since about 1970 there has been a really tremendous opening-up. A few years ago most students were at least on the surface cynical or apathetic about Christianity. Now I find almost everywhere a terrific eagerness to know more, and to find out about Jesus. The meetings are better attended, and far more people take a positive position. The Jesus Movement, and all that goes with it, has certainly helped. No one believes any longer that you have to be a dull, drab conformist to be a Christian. Quite a lot of this interest is "experience" centred, I agree. They want to know what Christ can "give" them, in the sense of awareness or a "lift" in enjoyment of life. But I don't feel that matters too much if what they are offered is the real thing, with all the consequences of Christian commitment spelt out.

The Festival of Light has, of course, taken over many of the features of the Jesus Movement—the chanting, the Jesus sign and so on. I like it, I admit, and I enjoy it, but I must say something in me wants to draw the line at Jesus stickers. I suppose the chanting is simply a modern form of the "responses" we have in the Prayer Book. Like them, it will probably become stereotyped into a ritual one day, but at the moment it adds a bit of zest and enthusiasm to Christian gatherings. The raised finger—"One Way to

Jesus"—has been misunderstood by the Press, who seem to regard it as a Nazi-style gesture. I can't think why. I like to think of it as saying that we are giving God the glory. I think that's what Larry Norman, who "invented it", really intended it to say.

Part of the value of the Festival of Light has been to encourage Christians to go out and share their faith with others, instead of sitting in our churches waiting for them to come to us. Arthur Blessitt really challenged me over this. When I heard him talking about Christian "witness" I felt condemnation poured over my head. Every time he stopped on the motorway for coffee, and every time he chatted with anyone on the street, he would talk to them about Jesus. Well, I've been down the motorway thousands of times, and often stopped for coffee. I've chatted with people there, and in other places. But unless they've raised the subject themselves I haven't talked to them about Christianity. "I've got to think out my whole position again," I said to myself, after hearing Arthur Blessitt speaking. "Perhaps my whole approach has been too oblique, too apologetic." But when I thought it over, I doubted if that was really so. After all, if I button-holed people in the street or in a motorway cafeteria and said, "Jesus loves you," it might or might not be a good "witness", but it definitely wouldn't be *me*. Probably the great need is for each of us to "do our thing" sensitively and happily, rather than strive to be like someone else, even such an incredible character as Arthur Blessitt.

9

Being Famous

I suppose one day I shall sit down for a meal in a restaurant and nobody will recognise me. The waitress won't want my autograph, and the people at the other tables won't peep over their shoulders and nudge each other.

Although I sometimes complain about it at present I think, deep down, if I'm honest, I'll miss it a bit!

It's funny now, looking back to the Summer of 1958, just before "Move It"—our first hit record—broke. I was working in the office of a factory at Enfield and playing clubs and pubs in the evenings. We went everywhere by bus and Green Line coach, humping our equipment with us.

But since "Move It" and the "Oh Boy!" TV shows, I've never once been on a bus in Britain, or a tube train. It's just impossible! Even having a meal in an ordinary restaurant can be embarrassing. When I'm driving the car and stop at traffic lights, people wind down the windows of their cars and wave or shout. If I walk down the street complete strangers stop me for an autograph.

I realise it's the same for everybody whose face is well known, and it probably explains why showbiz people tend to keep to themselves in a clique, and spend most of their time in the "in" showbiz clubs and eating places. But, although we all complain about it, human beings naturally love to be admired and noticed, and secretly we'd probably be disappointed if nobody took any notice of us!

A more serious result of being famous is the effect on people who were your friends. I remember that when I got well known my old friends from school and the estate, and even some of my relatives, became very awkward and embarrassed and stayed away from us. When my mother asked them why, they'd say, "Oh, we didn't think you'd be wanting us round *now*." Some pretended not to know whether to call me by my real name, "Harry", or my new name, "Cliff". In almost every case—there are just a couple of exceptions—the friends I had before felt there was a barrier grown up between us. It wasn't of my making, honestly: but they felt it, and our friendships couldn't survive this feeling of "difference" between us. Even now, a lot of people I meet obviously find it hard to treat me like an ordinary human being. This results in the entertainer being forced to choose his friends and acquaintances from the showbiz world, and really cuts him off from ordinary life. I think this is bad.

I've never been very keen on the "in" crowd of showbiz, and have always been just as pleased to get home and relax as live it up in the West End. I have never wanted to restrict my friendships just to showbiz people; and one of the special pleasures of my life now is that I have dozens of friends who are school teachers or solicitors or work in offices, and so on.

Fans can be a bit of a problem to the artist sometimes, too. Most of them are just people who like your work, buy your records and perhaps indulge in a bit of mild hero-worship. I was like that in my teens—I remember how I felt about Debbie Reynolds, for instance! But some of them go much further, and this I don't go along with.

Occasionally, the fan gets emotionally involved— even obsessed—with the artist. Sometimes they get so that they can't think about anything else. They even become very rude, funnily enough, saying things like, "If you don't answer the letter I wrote, I'll turn to hating you." Or they do crazy things, spending all their money trailing you across Britain (and beyond!) and hanging around wherever you go.

This may seem flattering, but I think it's unhealthy, and I've never encouraged it. For their own sake, I feel fans should keep their feet on the ground, have other interests and not get obsessed with the artist. One wrote to me, "You're the only thing that makes life worth while." That's a terrible thing to say about any human being, especially someone you don't really know at all. I would want to say to her now, "Only Jesus Christ can do that for you. Don't waste your time on me!"

I know there have been cases where promoters have exploited fans, and some fan clubs have been run almost as business enterprises by the artist's management. Actually our fan club—which closed down in

1967—was started and run independently, by a girl called Jan Vane, who launched it before we even *had* any management.

I suppose the artist has to expect to put up with the smaller things, like being approached on the beach on holiday and asked for an autograph; but it's that sort of thing that drives showbiz people to holidaying in far-away places. For years, I took my holidays in Portugal, in a private spot used very largely by showbiz people.

On the other hand, being famous has its compensations. When I finally quit show business, I shall miss quite a lot of little things—being able to ring up and get tickets for any show, going to first nights and premières, being able to get suits made quickly and that sort of thing. I've seen most of the world, and met many fascinating people, of course.

But these things don't matter all that much to me now. I can honestly say I'd give them up tomorrow if I felt the time had come to do another job, like teaching; and I don't think I'd miss them seriously at all.

I enjoy being well known, I suppose, as I think anybody would. But I've tried not to get emotionally involved with fame, and I hope I can say goodbye to it without tears and without regrets.

10

My Favourite Book

I used to say *Wuthering Heights* was my favourite book. I thought I would like to play Heathcliff in a film of it! But that was partly because it's the only book I can remember reading more than once: I think I read it three times.

I like science fiction, too—that goes with my love of SF films, I suppose. The best one I have read, if you can call it science fiction, is Aldous Huxley's *Brave New World*. I wouldn't say I'm a great reader, but I've come across a book that is very much older than Huxley's or *Wuthering Heights*, and which I can now confidently say is my favourite book. It is the Bible.

I've never been an atheist—I've always believed in something, and I used to call the something "God". That's the position of lots of people who have a nominal sort of religion. I sometimes prayed, usually selfishly, but since I was a boy I'd never read the Bible at all.

For one thing, I was busy—busy getting into show-biz, busy getting to the top. Then, I couldn't see what this old, old book had to say to a modern young person like myself. It never occurred to me that a book thousands of years old had anything important or relevant to say to me in 1962.

Then, when I was on tour in Australia with the Shads, I told Brian Locking, our lead guitarist, that I was thinking of going to a séance to "get in touch" with my dad, who had died the previous year. He was definitely against it: I asked him why, and he simply said it was wrong and began reading bits from the Bible to me. I was really shaken to find one of my friends took the Bible so seriously. Not only that, but it seemed to make sense. I decided to try reading it myself.

I began with the Gospels—Matthew, Mark, Luke and John—in the New Testament. I found it fantastically interesting. I mean that. I read chapter after chapter! When I was on tour in South Africa, about an hour before the show each day, I would run a bath and then lie in the hot water reading on and on. I read all four Gospels, and then Acts.

Mind you, a bit later I made a big mistake; the sort of mistake that could lead some people to give up reading the Bible altogether. That was when I decided to read through the whole Bible from start to finish.

I began with Genesis. That was great—the Creation, the Flood, Abraham and so on. Then came Exodus: the first twenty chapters were fine—the Hebrews leaving Egypt and the giving of the Ten Commandments. But after that I got slowed down in the building of the Tabernacle. I plodded on, but gave up in Deuteronomy. What *is* it all about? I asked myself.

That experience put me off the Old Testament for a

while, but fortunately it didn't put me off reading the Bible altogether.

What I learnt then was that we all need help in reading the Bible. We need God's help. That's why we should pray as we read that He will help us to grasp the truth He has put there. But we also need human help in understanding the actual words, just exactly what it says and means.

Sometimes I'm asked, "How should I set about reading the Bible seriously for the first time?"

Assuming the person who asks this question is not yet a committed Christian, I would advise him to start by reading John's Gospel. Here he will come up against the amazing personality of Jesus Christ. I honestly believe He is irresistible and that you just *can't* ignore Him.

As you read the New Testament you are forced to face up to a tremendously important question: "Either Jesus Christ was a fool or a liar, or else He was what He said He was—the Son of God."

If you decide He was a fool or liar, then presumably you won't bother reading any more. If you decide He was telling the truth when He said He was the Son of God, then you'll go on reading, getting help, studying with others and finding out more. If you do, there can't be any doubt that, in the end, you will find an even better reason for believing in Him as the Son of God. You will come to know Him personally and trust Him for yourself. The Bible is like that: once you come to grips with it, you can't shake off its truth.

But most people won't come to grips with it. The general attitude of ordinary people is to ridicule the Bible, tear it to pieces and say it's full of contradictions and so on. But most of them have never made a serious attempt to read it.

During the last five or six years, I've been in endless discussions and friendly arguments, mostly with show-biz people, about religion, God, life after death and so on. When we've been filming, or doing a long panto-mime run, it's amazing how often our off-stage conversation has got round to those sorts of subject.

Now what happens in these conversations, or arguments, is that everybody chips in with his or her own ideas and theories. It's surprising the fantastic and superstitious theories people produce—reincarnation, ghosts, spiritualism and plenty of weirder things too! Then somebody would ask me what I thought.

I would say, "Well, the Bible says . . ." and they'd listen politely while I tried to explain what the Bible had to say, so far as I knew, on the subject. When I'd finished, someone would say, "Oh, I can't agree with *your ideas*, Cliff. I prefer so-and-so's." It was no good explaining that they weren't *my* ideas at all, but God's. So far as they were concerned, the craziest or weirdest idea from a science-fiction story was just as valid as the Word of God. Christians have to keep on emphasising that the Bible is their authority. We must prove its worth, its inspiration, its authority and its truth.

The trouble is, however much they may admire an

individual Christian's faith, people are unsympathetic to the idea of a definite authority lying behind it. In other words, they admire a faith but neglect the basis on which it is founded. So far as Christians are concerned, in the words of an important Report of a Church of England Conference in 1967, "to differ from the Bible is to deviate from the truth".

Of course, many people were turned against the Bible by ghastly RI lessons at school, when the Bible was read but not explained, or else was taught as though it was very boring history. But sometimes, years later, they have picked up the Bible, perhaps in a new translation, and been "captured" by it.

I think it's a pity that school RI concentrates so much on the Old Testament—Samuel, Moses and so on—because if that's all people get of the Bible they're missing the heart of it, Jesus Christ. RI shouldn't be history or culture, but concentrate on men who changed the world, Jesus Christ and the apostles.

Of course, lots of the Old Testament is very important, especially things like the account of the creation and the Ten Commandments. For one thing, they are essential for understanding why Christ came into the world. For the same reason, some of the Old Testament prophecies about the coming Messiah (Christ) should be taught. But I'm sure for most people who are not yet Christians the Gospels and the Acts of the Apostles will be the most interesting parts of the Bible.

Sometimes people ask me how I personally go

about reading the Bible. For a long while after I became a Christian I used the Scripture Union method, which I think is a very good idea for those beginning to read the Bible seriously.

The Scripture Union provides you with a little booklet, which gives you a short Bible reading for each day and some notes by an expert explaining any difficulties and pointing out important things in the passage which you might otherwise miss. I believe there are one or two other similar schemes for Bible reading.

During the Summer of 1972 I took a break from work and did some really serious study at Oak Hill Theological College, in North London. It's a college where they train Anglican clergymen, but that doesn't mean I'm thinking of being ordained. Really I just felt the need, after several years of speaking at Christian meetings and rallies, to get to know the Bible and Christian doctrine a great deal better. After all, there comes a time when the story of how you got "converted" begins to get a bit dated, and when you can't any longer fend off awkward questions by saying you're only a beginner.

I think I can say my studies have done me a lot of good. In fact, in one sense they've changed my faith. I've always felt that my faith was solidly based, but actually to sit down and concentrate on a deeper study of the Bible and to find just *how* solid it all is was a tremendous experience. I was amazed at how consistent the Bible is, from start to finish, and how frivolous some of the objections to it really are.

Anyway, one of the things I had to do during this course was to summarise the argument of each chapter of the Epistle to the Romans in five lines. I thought I knew Romans quite well. When I first wrote this book in 1968 I said that I'd just read Romans and found it "tremendous". I also said that I'd been reading about a couple of chapters at a time. But now I found what it means really getting to grips with the book. It took me five hours to write the notes on one chapter, and then I simply couldn't summarise it in five lines, or anything like it.

I used to read in the New English Bible translation of the New Testament, but now I am using the Revised Standard Version, which is another modern translation of the whole Bible. I think it's important to use a modern version, so that you don't get caught out by obscure sentences or discouraged by reading but not understanding.

There are sure to be difficulties in reading the Bible. There are in any book which has anything important or serious to say. When I come to a difficulty I make a note of it and then ask somebody. Sometimes there isn't any answer, in the sense that nobody can be absolutely sure what the saying means. I remember querying Christ's reference to "two swords" as He and the disciples were going into the Garden of Gethsemane on the night He was betrayed. Nobody can really explain what He meant; though perhaps if we could have been there and heard His tone of voice and seen His expression, it would have been perfectly obvious.

At any rate, it would be daft to let the difficulties put us off or stop us reading more.

In any case, the difficulties in the Gospels aren't in the actual words, but in their deep implication. Often you can read a sentence on different levels and get different meanings from it.

Most of the sayings of Christ aren't really very difficult—it is accepting them that's so hard! It would be wonderful to "turn the other cheek" if we could bring ourselves to do it.

The saying of Paul about "burning coals" bugged me for a while. He says, "If your enemy is hungry, feed him: if he is thirsty, give him drink; for by so doing you will heap burning coals upon his head."* I thought hard about that one, and asked several people how they understood it. In the end I came to the conclusion that what Paul was saying was really something that is true to life and experience: if you can be nice to someone who hates you, you make him see how unreasonably he is behaving. I'm sure there have been many conversions through Christians loving people who hated them.

Some people make a lot out of supposed contradictions between the four Gospel writers. For me, the different accounts are not contradictory, but each writer adds details to fill out the picture of Christ: one emphasises one thing, another misses that, but fills in another detail.

For myself, I believe every word of the New Testa-

* See Romans 12:20.

ment, and everything it says I accept. This really fol-
lows logically from my belief in Jesus as the Son of
God : the New Testament consists of His words and
the words of the apostles. He called and instructed. So
far as the Old Testament is concerned, there are certainly more difficulties, but I believe it is the Word of
God and that if we understood it perfectly the difficulties would disappear.

11

Things I Get Asked

In this chapter, I've lumped together a lot of questions I've been asked from time to time which mostly only need short answers.

You're very rich. Doesn't the Bible say rich people can't get into heaven?

No, it does not. It says that it's easier for a camel to go through the eye of a needle than for those who *trust in riches* to enter the kingdom of heaven. Saint Paul said of the church at Corinth that it had "not many" rich members—not "none"!

Well, I certainly don't "trust in riches". I suppose I am rich, but money doesn't bother me. I have never asked how much I'd be paid for a show. And, while I'd miss my Jensen and my comfortable house, I can honestly say that living on, say, a teacher's salary, wouldn't disturb me at all. After all, I *do* know what it is to be hard up—I wasn't born rich, by any means.

Actually, to be rich is a great and serious responsibility for the Christian, because money is a powerful thing, for good or evil. I try to see that my money is used wisely and well. I can't say more than that.

Showbiz life is supposed to be very immoral. Does it shock you?

I really don't know for sure that showbiz people are any more immoral than bank clerks or bus drivers. I suppose they're more casual about sex and take marriage too lightly on the whole, but to depict the showbiz world as a great sink of iniquity is a terrible exaggeration. There are plenty of highly moral and good-living people in the entertainment world.

But, of course, there is immorality, it can't be denied. No, I'm not shocked by it. No Christian should be shocked by sin, because the Bible tells us that it's the logical result of man's rebellion against God. People have been sinning since the Fall, so there's not much point in being shocked by it.

That doesn't mean I approve of it. I think Christians have been too tolerant, too scared to speak out in case people should think they were weird or cranky. I don't mean we should be intolerant of *people* who do things we consider to be wrong; but that we should be intolerant—as Jesus was—of evil, cruelty, injustice, exploitation and so on. We need to say clearly when we feel something is wrong. I think people respect us more when we show we know what we believe and aren't afraid to say so.

Do you think you are being exploited by Christians?

No, definitely not. I make up my own mind about what I do and where I appear, and nobody has ever tried to put any pressure on me to speak at a meeting, or anything like that. What I've done, like singing and speaking at Christian meetings, I've done completely voluntarily, because I've felt it to be my Christian duty to tell people about this wonderful thing I've discovered.

If "Cliff Richard" can be used to take Christianity to people, or bring people to hear about Christ, then I'm happy about it. I'm not ramming it down anybody's throat: they can come, hear for themselves, and make up their own minds. Actually, I count it a great privilege to be able to do this sort of thing.

Where do you think your career is going?

I don't know! What I do know is that it has changed. After ten years or more as primarily a Top Ten singer, I suppose I've moved on now to a more settled kind of career, though still centred, of course, on singing.

The one disappointment has been over acting. I would still love to do more "serious" acting, but I know in my heart of hearts that if I'm to do it I shall have to give up everything else for a year, and work at it from the repertory level upwards. But I'm not willing to do that, at the moment, so the acting part of my career has rather ground to a halt.

I would love to have been in "Godspell", because of what it says. So many plays and musicals nowadays are negative. But I should not have wanted to be in "Superstar", for reasons I've already set out. Mind you, I wasn't offered parts in either, anyway!

I think the best acting I've done so far was in Graham Greene's "The Potting Shed", which I was in at the Sadler's Wells Theatre with the Bromley Rep. We were there because the theatre at Bromley was burnt down just before we were due to open. "The Potting Shed" is a beautifully written, positive and sensitive sort of play. I only wish we'd had a longer run. Strangely enough, we had rather better reviews than the original West End run twenty years ago, but that may simply be because people are more willing nowadays to accept a play with an explicitly Christian theme.

Do you consider yourself a conformist?

People who ask that are usually implying that to be a Christian and not be living it up is a terribly respectable and boring way of life. They think that because I prefer hymns to hashish I'm a conformist.

This just shows how wrong you can be. A conformist is somebody who decides his beliefs, tastes and actions according to what other people think, rather than abiding by his own convictions.

Most people think of the Beatles as being way-out non-conformists.

Several years ago, I remember talking to John Lennon about our favourite artists. I said I'd always admired Ray Charles.

"I used to," replied John, "until everyone else started liking him."

Now that really shook me. Probably he thinks differently now, but I reckoned then—and still do—that it's dreadful to change your opinion just because people will think you're a conformist otherwise. Really, that *is* being a conformist—not saying what you really believe but what you think will make an impression.

I'm all in favour of being a non-conformist, but I wouldn't change my opinion just to be different from everybody else, or to appear different.

In showbiz there's no doubt being a Christian and living a moral sort of life is a non-conformist thing to do. Actually, since I publicly said that I was a Christian quite a lot of showbiz people have sidled up to me and said, "I'm a Christian, too, but I haven't the nerve to tell everybody." Some of them have been really top people. But to keep quiet because of what people would think is to be "conformist". To speak out is, surely, "non-conformist".

I please myself where things like music, clothes or food are concerned. If I see some gear I like, then I'll wear it. If there's an artist whose music I take to, I'll say so. I don't wait to find out what everybody else is thinking first.

Perhaps the *New Musical Express* can answer this question for me! Norrie Drummond said in an article, "By show business standards, Cliff Richard must be one of the most non-conformist artists around." So there!

Have you ever disliked one of your own records? Or shows? Or films?

No, not really. I've liked some more than others, but I've never recorded a song I didn't like.

One of my biggest hits, "Living Doll", I didn't like at first. In the film it was made for, it was played at a different tempo and with a different backing. When we came to record it, I suggested we tried a different tempo. The result was really a different song altogether and a really huge hit. The film version has never appealed to me, but the recorded version I liked very much.

It's been the same with most of my work. I can't say that I've *hated* anything I've done professionally, but obviously, looking back, there are things I'd do differently now. I looked pretty gormless on the old "Oh Boy!" shows, and I can't stand watching myself in "The Young Ones". Naturally, I wouldn't perform in the "Oh Boy!" style now—practically nobody does, anyway!—but I don't strongly dislike it.

My favourites are harder to pick out. For different reasons I like different records. "The Day I Met Marie" is one of my favourites. It's very different from most of the others, and I suppose I wouldn't have recorded a song like this earlier in my career. Another favourite was a song recorded several years ago, "The Twelfth of Never". Neither of these two songs got to the top of the Hit Parade!

Do you like performing on television?

TV is a fabulous medium, with tremendous impact, but it can "kill" an artist who makes too many appearances. Most of us owe a lot to TV in making our work known. In a sense, television "made" Cliff Richard and the Drifters (as we were then).

It's really quite funny to see that in this book in 1968 I said that half a dozen TV appearances a year was the ideal number. "More than that, and one may suffer from over-exposure." Well, I must be suffering badly, because I've had several long-running TV series since then.

Actually, what I've decided is that series don't count as appearances!

Our TV series for the BBC have drawn fantastic audiences—something between twelve and fifteen million people a week. It has been these series more than anything else that have moved me on from being a Top Ten disc artist to being something of a family entertainer. It's probably also because of the TV shows that our live concerts are still full.

Incidentally, unlike most TV performers I have to learn my linking script, because without glasses I can't read the autocue! I tried contact lenses, but they didn't really suit me from the comfort point of view.

Have you made records in other languages?

I have made several records in German, and one or two in French, Spanish and Italian. I don't suppose the accent is very good, but I get by!

Usually I perform in English in other countries. Beat music is universal anyway, I find, and the sound of most pop songs can be enjoyed even if you can't understand the words.

What was your favourite performance?

That's an easy one! I enjoyed making the film "Two a Penny" more than anything.

For me, it was a wonderful opportunity to combine a long ambition to try my hand at a strong "dramatic" role in a film, and also a desire to use whatever gifts God had given me, with experience in the cause of Christianity.

I talked it over with Peter Gormley, my manager. He gave me some good advice. He wanted me to regard the "Billy Graham film" (as we called it then) as part of my professional career, and I agreed with him. I was due to make a film that Summer (1966)— "Finders Keepers"—but I made a firm agreement with Frank and Jim that I would do the World Wide film the following Summer (1967).

An English writer who lives in California, Stella Linden, wrote a very good screen play and we actually shot some footage for the film at a couple of Crusade meetings that June.

As I got to know Jim Collier, and the screen play, I was more and more excited about this film, which was now called "Two a Penny". Jim is a fantastic director, the best I have ever worked with and, if you think I'm biased, ask the team who made the picture with him in 1967. He was determined to do an honest, provocative and real film, and he sold his enthusiasm to me.

My part was that of a light-fingered, bed-hopping materialist, supposed to be studying fashion at Art College but actually more interested in earning a quick fiver or two either by singing in pubs or doing shady little deals in narcotics. As you will see, that's about as far from the part I played in, say, "Summer Holiday" or "Finders Keepers" as you could get! I suppose you could also say it's quite a little way from the sort of person I really am.

This character—Jamie—has two females in tow, his mum (played by Dora Bryan) and his bird, Carol (played by Ann Holloway). The film isn't about drugs, or singing, or even romance, however. It's really a depth study of what happens to two bright, swinging young people when the Christian message (by courtesy of Billy Graham) starts to poke its way into their situation. In fact, they're only swinging on the outside, and their inner reactions to Christ, and to each other, really make the film.

I can honestly say I had more fun and more satisfaction making "Two a Penny" than out of any other thing I've ever done in showbiz. Although the film was made on a shoe-string—it's a million-pound film made for less than a quarter of that!—and almost entirely shot on location, it would be impossible to imagine a happier atmosphere to work in.

I've been in a few films, you know, and I've seen how delays and frustrations, like bad weather on location, can upset people and lead to tantrums, tempers and rudeness. We had our share of delays and frustrations in "Two a Penny" all right—six weeks on location and two weeks in a tiny studio designed for making TV commercials guaranteed that—but there were no tempers, tantrums or rudeness.

Most of the team had been together before, making "Alfie" and "Khartoum", and they were a great crowd, but I think everybody agreed it was Jim Collier who made the difference. If ever Christianity was lived out in front of people, this was it.

So you see why I say "Two a Penny" was my favourite performance. Everything about doing it was great—my first Christian film (even though I play an atheist in it!), my first dramatic role, working under a Christian director and working with the happiest crowd of people imaginable. Although it was desperately hard work—I reckon I was doing a sixty-hour week during the filming—I can say I enjoyed every minute of it.

Do you believe in prayer?

Yes, I do. To me it's part and parcel of being a Christian.

Long before I was a Christian I used to pray sometimes, but usually it was purely selfish, for something I wanted.

Christian prayer is completely different. It is communication with God. I can pray anywhere, any time. It isn't just asking God for things, though that's included, but also sharing in God's interest and work in the world; letting Him shape my interests; seeking His will and asking His help for other people. For instance, I pray for my family, the boys in my Crusader class and so on.

It may sound pious, but I get more satisfaction out of praying for others. It's not only more "blessed", but it's more fun, too. There is nothing a Christian is short of, but he longs to share what he has with others.

I always pray at night, before going to bed, but also at other times. I don't have a set formula of prayer, but I believe it should be a constant activity of the Christian. Someone said to me once that the day should be given at its start "to the Lord". The only way you can be sure that you *have* given it to Him is to be conscious of the fact that each action has begun with a brief offering to God—and that is prayer. In these terms, I pray for everything, practically everything. As soon as you think of God in conjunction with what you are doing, or going to do, that's praying.

At the Palladium, during the "Cinderella" run, I used to pray like that about the coming performance, while I was making up. I didn't pray that it would be a "good" one, but I sort of "brought God in on it"—"gave" it to Him, you could say.

I also think it's important to pray with other Christians whenever one can. This is something many churchgoers have never done—just to meet with a few other Christians and pray on any subject quite informally. Of course, we also pray together in our services of worship, but this informal coming together to pray has a special quality of unity about it.

I must admit I still get knocked out when God answers my prayers! I think, "That's lucky!" and then realise, "But of course I prayed about it!" We shouldn't be surprised, I suppose, when God does what He had promised to do, but being human I imagine we just reckon it is all too good to be true.

What do you think about the modern teenager?

Well, I stopped being one several years ago, of course, so I'm not speaking from personal, up to date experience.

On the whole, I think people underrate today's teenagers. Many older folk think that all teenagers are drug-takers, or violent, or beatniks or all three at once! They read of a teenage riot somewhere and then conclude that all teenagers are like this. That means millions of kids are being condemned because of a handful of stupid and bad ones.

I know of hundreds of teenagers who are doing

tremendous things—serving the community, helping old people, doing voluntary service overseas and so on. It is ridiculous to label them all as hooligans.

My biggest disappointment is that many teenagers just aren't interested in Christianity and don't want to know about it. But hundreds of thousands of youngsters *are* interested, and many churches are full of teenagers. And Christians are trying desperately hard nowadays to reach the ones who are still "outside".

Does God guide you ... and how?

When people ask this, they usually mean, "Can God help me to make right decisions and steer me through difficult periods in my life?"

I believe definitely that God *does* guide us, without a doubt, but perhaps not quite in the way people mean it who ask this question.

The way I see it, the basic Christian commitment is to tell God you want to do things His way, not your own, in future. You believe He has heard and answered that prayer, and so you accept *whatever comes* as being His will for you. Even if what comes is not what you expected or wanted, yet still God *is* guiding and still it *is* His will.

I suppose a psychiatrist could explain all this away, but to me it's a matter of simple faith. If God has promised to guide His people (and He has*), then if you sincerely want to do His will He *does* guide you,

* Proverbs 3 : 5, 6.

even when it doesn't seem like it.

But does God guide every *detail* of our daily lives?

Here, I think the basic thing is that (according to the Bible) nothing happens to the Christian by accident. Saint Paul says that "in *everything* God works for good with those who love Him".* We may think we are choosing to do things, and we are; but God knows in advance what we will choose. If we pray for His guidance it shows we want to do His will, and we are aligning ourselves with His plan for us. To accept that we are responsible for our actions, and yet that God knows all about us and plans our lives for us, is hard. But to accept both these things is the basis of humility, of giving *myself* to God. I am responsible, and yet I am completely dependent.

What do you think about war?

Until a short time ago I had never thought about this seriously, beyond the usual things—being against violence and so on. But I've been asked about war, and especially about Vietnam, so often that I've had to think it through.

I suppose now I would have to call myself a pacifist. At least, I believe as a Christian I should be against war, *any* war, for any purpose. It seems inconsistent to follow Christ, who said, "Love your enemies," and then go out to kill them.

Having said that, I just hope I would have the

* Romans 8:28 (RSV).

courage of that conviction if a time ever came when it was put to the test—say, by being called up to defend this country against attack.

What do you look for in a girl?

I hate answering that question, because it implies a sort of cold, calculating approach to people. Mainly, I like a girl to be reserved. I don't mean that her personality should be submerged but that she isn't pushing or showing off to get attention.

I like girls to be natural, neat and tidy, lively and interesting as *people*. And nowadays I have to add that I could never marry a girl who was not a practising Christian.

Are you ambitious?

There was a time when work ruled my life completely. All I wanted to do was make records, and the end of the world was around the corner if one of them didn't get into the top five.

The trouble is, the more success you have, the more you want. It's only natural. While success keeps on coming, you feel fantastic. But what happens when it stops? Ambition has to snowball all the time.

Now my attitude has changed. The best way to stop ambition from eating you up is to have an interest outside your work; and this I have. I hope I work as hard these days as I ever have, and I'm still "ambitious" in the sense that I want to do everything as well as I possibly can. But my attitude and my motive have changed completely.

My attitude has changed because I believe I have a healthier mental approach to work. Life is so much easier when you haven't got anything dragging on your mind. If and when anything goes wrong, it's not one hundred per cent important to me any more. I try to look at the failure objectively and iron out the mistakes.

This has involved learning to accept criticism—something I've never found easy! In fact, I'm still learning . . .

My motive has changed, too. The Bible says *whatever* you do you should do it "heartily"* and "in the name of the Lord Jesus".† I reckon that "whatever" includes everything, not just religious things, but recording sessions, TV performances, filming and so on. My motive is to do it well, for Christ's sake. I'm not claiming I always succeed, needless to say, but even trying really *does* change your approach to it, believe me!

What are the biggest difficulties you face in being a Christian?

Apart from those everybody has, within myself, I suppose it's the thing that keeps coming out in this

* Colossians 3 : 23.
† Colossians 3 : 17.

book. Most Christians live their lives privately and quietly. Nobody praises them much for the good they do, and nobody cuts them up when they fail or make fools of themselves. Well-known Christians, like Billy Graham, the Archbishop of Canterbury and so on, are people who have great maturity and experience. As Christians, they began in obscurity and later became well known.

But people like me *begin* well known, before we've got the Christian maturity or experience to cope with it. Obviously that brings problems. Other Christians of my age or experience can say stupid things, make mistakes, let Christ down—and it's a matter between themselves, a few other people and God. But when I say stupid things and so on, it's public knowledge: millions of people are in on it.

I'm *not* complaining, but I suppose that is my biggest personal problem as a Christian.

12

The Next Big Event

Showbiz people, as I've said already, are a rather superstitious lot, and many of them pick up fantastic theories about life after death, reincarnation, ghosts and so on. Sometimes I get asked what I think the future holds.

That's a question I can't answer, because what's the use of saying what I *think* about something nobody knows anything about? I reckon there are too many wild and cranky ideas about already!

But I'm always prepared to repeat what the Bible says, as I understand it, about the future, the end of the world, life after death and so on. These aren't "Cliff's ideas", but what God has revealed.

Obviously the world must end one day, perhaps soon. From the Bible I do not see any hope of the world getting better and better until Christ has returned.

That will be the world's next really big event—the return of Jesus Christ. When He went back to heaven the disciples stood looking up into the sky. As they watched, amazed, an angel told them that "this Jesus, who was taken up from you into heaven, will come in the same way as you saw Him go into heaven."*

* Acts 1:11 (RSV).

When Christ returns, this world as we know it will end. The earth will disintegrate in flames and heat, and God will bring in a new heaven and a new earth.* Nobody knows the timing of these events, but the Bible makes it clear that they will all happen. Before they do, and before the return of Christ, which will begin this train of events, other prophecies of His coming will have to be fulfilled. There will be false Christs, major wars and other troubles, and the gospel will have to be preached throughout the whole world.†

But then Christ will come, in one blinding moment of truth. Everybody will know—this will not be a secret visit.‡ Many people will be amazed and terrified, but it will not be a disaster for those under Christ, because this tremendous event is going to happen for the best. It will be the beginning of a whole new world!

Some people may say, "How can you be so sure this will happen?"

The way I see it, if all the Bible's prophecies that related to events now passed have come true, then it's reasonable to assume its prophecies related to future events will come true as well. The fact is, *all* the prophecies related to events now past—the coming of Christ, His birth, death and resurrection, the dispersal and suffering of the Jews and so on—have come true, although they were written down centuries before

* 2 Peter 3:7–13.   † Matthew 24:6, 7, 14, 24.
‡ Matthew 24:27.

they happened! So it seems foolish to pretend that the Bible's prophecies about what still lies in the future won't prove equally accurate.

Perhaps my generation will be alive on earth when Christ returns. Perhaps we won't be. If we are not, it won't really matter. You see, the Bible teaches that whether we are alive or dead ("asleep" is Saint Paul's word) at Christ's coming, we shall be "changed" in the twinkling of an eye.

You can read all about it in 1 Corinthians 15, verses 51–58; some of the words are included in the spiritual "We Shall be Changed", which I sang on my *Good News* LP.

"We shall not all sleep," says Paul, "but we shall be changed, in a moment, in the twinkling of an eye, at the last trumpet ... For this perishable nature must put on the imperishable, and this mortal nature must put on immortality."*

That means that after I die, the next thing I shall really know is the "trumpet" sounding for the resurrection, and all the Christian dead will rise and be given new, immortal bodies and natures and live with Christ for ever.

That's why I *know* there is life after death. God has promised it in the Bible. I don't know what form that life will take, but I know it will happen; and I know it will be good. But, frankly, I wouldn't want to face the future, and especially the end of the world, without Jesus Christ. He alone makes the prospects good.

* RSV.

13

The Biggest Step

The biggest step you can take is from life into death. Or *vice versa*.

I took the step from death to life six or seven years ago, when I became a Christian. Jesus Christ said, "He who hears my word and believes Him who sent me, has eternal life; he does not come into judgment, but has passed from death to life."

"From death to life"—that's a huge step. In this chapter I want to explain exactly how it could happen to you, or me, or anybody.

There are three stages in this process of becoming a Christian.

The first stage is realising the state we are in. The second is realising that we need to get out of that state. The third is realising the way it can be done.

The first stage is the most painful one. In this, we have to face up to the fact of sin and how serious it is when the Bible says, "All have sinned and fall short of the glory of God."

You see, sin is *huge*, because it separates us from God. By sin, I don't just mean wrong actions, but intentions and thoughts, too.

Jesus said in the Sermon on the Mount that the Commandment which says, "Thou shalt do no murder" also includes anger and hate. The Command-ment that says, "Thou shalt not commit adultery" in-cludes looking at a woman lustfully (what He called "adultery in the heart").

In other words, sin is an *inner* thing which destroys us and cuts us off from God : and we have *all* got it.

Now it's one thing to admit you're a "sinner"—though plenty of people deny it—but it's quite another to reach the stage of wanting to get out of that state.

This is what the Bible calls "conviction of sin", and it happens when the Holy Spirit begins to show us that we are sinners, and the consequences of sin. Then we want to break free from sin, but we find we can't. No matter how hard we try, we can't lick sin on our own : it's too deep in our natures.

The third stage (though they don't always happen in this order) is when we come to realise—or, rather, God shows us—that the only way out of this is through His Son, Jesus Christ.

How can Jesus Christ deal with our sins?

It is all to do with His death on the Cross. When He died there, He wasn't dying for His own sins, be-cause He never committed any, but for ours. He bore the brunt of all the sins that had been committed and would be committed in history. He paid the price for God to forgive them all. He sacrificed Himself so that the consequences of our sin could be removed.

When we have accepted His sacrifice for us, God forgives us all our past sins, and gives us eternal life. But He also gives us a new attitude to sin.

If I sin now, as a Christian, God will forgive me if I repent and confess my sin—He has promised to do this for Christ's sake. "If we (Christians) confess our sins, God is faithful and just and will forgive our sins and cleanse us from all unrighteousness."*

This is not a licence to sin as much as I like, but a procedure to cover sins which Christians, because of human weakness, may commit. God's plan for us is that we should live essentially sin-free lives. By knowing Christ we can have a new *attitude* to sin, that is the fundamental difference.

So, stepping from death to life is really stepping from sin into Christ. "He who has the Son has life; he who has not the Son of God has not life." There is the crucial difference—Christ. And there is the awful warning, too.

God offers us immortality, in Christ. But the Bible also warns of the terrible consequences of ignoring His offer. "He who has not the Son of God has not life." Christians believe there is an urgency about the gospel, and it is dangerous to shrug it off. There will come a day when it will be too late, and those without Christ will suffer the awful sensation of realising their state and the folly of having rejected Him.

Sometimes people say to me, "But I lead a decent life, do a charity show now and again and help old ladies across the road. Surely that makes it OK and I'll get into heaven?"

Well, according to the Bible, it doesn't. Christianity

* 1 John 1:9 (RSV).

isn't "do-goodery".

There's a girl called Valerie Hadert in a hospital near Brentwood, Essex. She's a tremendous Christian, although she is dreadfully handicapped and even has to spend some time in an iron lung. I reckon she's a wonderful writer of verse, and I've put one of her songs to music and have sung it many times. It really sums up the Christian answer to this sort of "do-good" idea of Christianity. The last verse points out that, in God's sight, even our "righteousnesses" are like "filthy rags",* so, she says, if you think what you've done makes you fit for heaven—"*think again*"!

Saint Paul said that we are saved by grace through faith—"not because of works, lest any man should boast".† If we could earn a place in heaven by things we did, we could justifiably boast of it—"I was good enough for heaven." But even our *best* actions aren't good enough for God, let alone our worst ones. We need salvation: we need to *be* saved, not to save ourselves. We need Christ; and that includes me—and you. It takes a very wilful person to reject Him, to turn away from Him. I know Him, because He's changed my life, and I'd like to think you might get to know Him too.

* Isaiah 64:6.
† Ephesians 2:9 (RSV).